The Power of Car...

How to create an awesome anir...
noticed and your message hea... ...

INDEX

PART 1 – WHY ARE CARTOONS SO POWERFUL?	2
The Special Sauce	2
Conditioned since Childhood to Love Cartoons	3
Lowering Your Guard	3
Seeing the Bigger Picture	6
The Power of Toon!	7
A Solid "What does/doesn't work" Formula	8
A Few Undeniable Facts	9
How to Create an Awesome Animated Video	14
PART 2 – HOW TO CREATE A COMPELLING SHORT STORY	15
The Secret Recipe	15
From Theory to Practice	19
Five Challenges	20
PART 3 – HOW TO CREATE AN AWESOME ANIMATED VIDEO CLIP:	
AN EASY 6-STEP PROCESS	28
Step 1 - Write an awesome Script or Short Story	28
Step 2 - Storyboard	29
Step 3 - Voiceover Guide / Background Music	32
Step 4 - Dividing the Slides	37
Step 5 - Populate the Slides with Visuals	47
Step 6 - Timing	59
A Real Insider Tip	61
IS THERE A SHORTCUT?	63
A PERSONAL NOTE FROM THE UNICORN	65
ABOUT THE AUTHOR	67
APPENDIX	68
Worksheet: Super Easy 5-Step Script Writing Template	69
Case Study: PowToon's Script for Startups Table	70

ALL RIGHTS RESERVED. This book contains material protected under International and Federal Copyright Laws and Treaties. All and any parts of this book that are reproduced or transmitted in any form or by any means, electronically or mechanically, including photocopying, recording, or by any information storage and retrieval system should clearly state details of the author / publisher.

Copyright
© 2013 Ilya Spitalnik www.PowToon.com

Part 1
WHY ARE CARTOONS SO POWERFUL?

The Special Sauce

Have you ever found yourself watching a cartoon where mice talk, elephants fly or penguins build airplanes and say to yourself: "That's ridiculous! Where'd they come up with such nonsense?"

Actually, no! The likelihood is you've never been bothered by how implausible a cartoon was...

Why? It's because something magical happens when you watch a cartoon. Psychologists have a fancy name for it: **"The Suspension of Disbelief"**

It's the special sauce that stops you from asking critical questions such as: Can this actually happen? Is this really possible? Does this make any sense?

Conditioned since Childhood to Love Cartoons

Most of us watched cartoons as children and still - to this day - associate them with childish, non-business, and (more importantly) non-sales related matters.

Basically, we've been conditioned to accept cartoons as a non-threatening form of communication and we absorb their messages in a very different way compared to the jaded "keep your guard up" attitude we typically adopt.

Lowering Your Guard

A cartoon encourages you to lower your guard and stop asking grown-up questions like: Do I like this packaging? Am I familiar with this brand? Do I have any prior experience with this vendor?

This is where cartoons become such a powerful marketing tool....

By eliminating the "criticizing" instinct for even just a few moments, we open ourselves to new messages.

To illustrate what I mean, take a look at these next two images. With each, be aware of the first thoughts that cross your mind:

Image 1

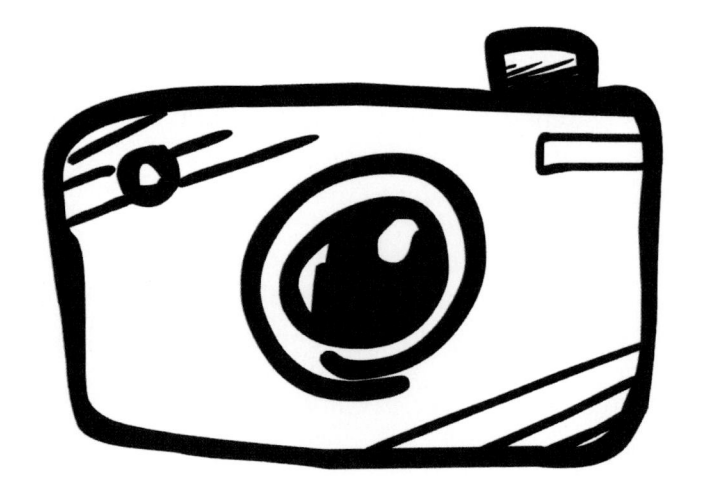

My thoughts:
"Oh, a camera - someone's probably taking a picture."

Image 2

My thoughts:
"Wow, that's a bit of a monster. Must be really heavy. You probably need special gear for that. I bet it costs a ton as well, it's probably intended more for professionals than for me."

Seeing the Bigger Picture

My "grown-up," detail-oriented approach to Image 2 makes it virtually impossible to see any kind of greater message someone may want to convey. I'm too caught up with the details to see the bigger picture (no pun intended).

Using the cartoon format adds a level of abstraction to the message that allows us to ignore petty details and concentrate on the greater message!

The Power of Toon!

Harnessing the power of a cartoon can help you create high-impact messages that speak to prospects in ways virtually no other medium can, because:

1. You're speaking to them via a channel they're conditioned to associate with fun and childhood (and most definitely *not* business and sales) - so their guard is down and they're massively more receptive.
2. The added level of abstraction allows them to focus on the **message** rather than petty details, so they can actually evaluate the real benefit.

If you'd like your audience to take note of what you have to say, there are few better ways than creating a cartoon to convey your message!

> Meet 'Retro-Phone' The next big thing!

A cartoon allows you to present an idea or product in a non-threatening, non-salesy, non-pushy way, because - after all - it's just a cutesey cartoon...

Granted, until recently, this process was prohibitively expensive, costing a minimum of $1,500 per minute and often reaching $25,000+ with professional animation studios.

This obstacle inspired me to shape PowToon's vision of creating a tool that makes it affordable for *anyone* to create animated clips for their business or service.

A Solid "What does/doesn't work" Formula

In this short book, I'm here to give you a solid **"What does/doesn't work" formula** for animated video clips (whether for your business or yourself), and provide a simple and incredibly effective recipe that will capture viewers' imagination, engage them, and inspire positive action towards you or your product.

In case the formula seems overly simplistic at first glance, let me emphasize that it is supported by a distilled analysis of **261,254** animated presentations and cartoons, or **PowToons** as we like to call them, which we surveyed to come up with one easy-to-use yet powerful recipe...

A Few Undeniable Facts

Before we start with the formula, let us review a few undeniable facts we've come to understand through empirical evidence and research:

1. STORIES SELL

It's no big secret that stories sell!

Customers don't want to be hit over the head with product features. They want to be sold a vision of how a particular product or service "will benefit me." They want to see themselves reaping rewards... ideally *lots* of them. Thing is, it can be difficult to create a "real life character" to convey a vision because of all the "grown-up" questions we would ask about this person. But it's incredibly easy to achieve a vision using a cartoon! Remember, a cartoon is all about the bigger picture and glossing over the details...

2. JOIN THE CONVERSATION IN THE VIEWER'S HEAD

Every one of us has a conversation going on in our head - ALL THE TIME!

Whenever we see anything, a subliminal debate wages within us, like in the earlier example of the cartoon vs. the real camera. Once you receive any sensory stimulus, your subconscious mind starts discussing it.

Therefore, in creating any story, we should aim to tap into that conversation going on in our prospects' head.

Not only that, but we must **establish a dialogue** with prospects to make them pay attention. I'll illustrate this principle further as we create our story.

3. IMAGES VS TEXT

Want viewers to pay attention with the logical part of the brain? Use speech. But if you want them to use the emotional faculty...use images! And if you want to fully engage viewers, **coordinate images and speech with music** to get the full impact of the logical and emotional sides.

Recognize that too much text in a presentation can be distracting. The human brain can process 275 words per minute in written form, and it can only hear 150 words per minute. This means that putting a lot of on-screen text can cause a mental disconnect.

Instead, "season" your cartoon with short phrases or words to emphasize emotional triggers. This can be a very powerful way of making your viewers pay attention at key moments in your presentation.

Tip: Keep your slides short and include lots of interesting visuals in your PowToon

Video Tip on using images: www.bit.ly/tip-images
Video Tip on using text: www.bit.ly/tip-text

4. BEST LENGTH FOR AN ANIMATED VIDEO CLIP

The average attention span of the Facebook generation is 90 seconds. This is the time you have to get your message across—and the first 7 seconds are the most crucial! That's when you have to convince viewers to actually continue watching.

Our research indicates…

Best cartoon length: 63-92 seconds

Critical start: 7-10 seconds

How many words should your script have?

Clip Length	Number of Words
30 seconds	85
60 seconds	160
90 seconds	230

So the maximum optimal length for an animated video is around 90 seconds, and you should aim to get viewers' attention - hook them - within the first 7 seconds. (As this is when they decide whether to continue listening or not).

5. SHORT - SHORTER - SHORTEST

It isn't easy to write a compelling short story. So it's okay to start out with a longer presentation, and then cutting it down. Draft your story, then read it through and edit out the non-essentials. Then read it through again, and cut it down some more, then rinse and repeat, until it is really, really short! (You can always add things back later).

The motto in writing your script is: short - shorter - shortest! This way, you can crystallize the essence of what you want to say and avoid losing viewers because you're too long-winded. An additional benefit is that it forces you to be very clear about what you want to convey.

How to Create an Awesome Animated Video

To create a short, punchy animated video, we need two things:

1. Create a compelling short story about the product or service—this serves as our animation script.

2. Turn this story into an awesome animated video clip using PowToon!

In Part 2 of this book, I'll lead you step-by-step through the creative process of drafting a simple, powerful script.

Then, in Part 3, I'll guide you through the actual animated video creation using the PowToon software.

PART 2
HOW TO CREATE A COMPELLING SHORT STORY

THE SECRET RECIPE

Captivate - Engage - Call to Action

Your objective is to create a story that leads viewers through the following 3 stages:

Stage 1: CAPTURE VIEWERS' ATTENTION

Stage 2: ENGAGE THEM LONG ENOUGH TO HEAR YOU OUT

Stage 3: INSPIRE POSITIVE ACTION TOWARDS YOU, YOUR BRAND or YOUR PRODUCT

Let's start creating a compelling story by asking three questions:

1. How do I capture viewers' attention in only 7 seconds?
2. How do I engage viewers so they'll want to hear us out?
3. How do I make them take action right here and now?

To make sure we're on the same page, let's clarify where your viewers will encounter your video: On the web? At a tradeshow? In your shop? Actually, it doesn't really matter! What matters is what they're thinking as they view your material. You have to enter the conversation in their heads...

Question 1
How do I capture the viewers' attention in only 7 seconds?

The first question viewers will be asking is: "Is this vendor talking to me? Is this content directed at me?"

So your first objective is to grab the viewers' attention and convince them that you're talking to them.

How do you do that?
Well, there are several ways. You can...

- shock them
- upset them
- make them laugh
- gross them out
- say something they really care about
- etc...

One of the more effective methods (and, incidentally, one that helps you qualify this person as a potential customer) is stating a problem that they're currently struggling with...i.e. a subject they really care about.

This will make them look up and pay attention!

You know your service or product best, and you know what problem(s) it solves. So state the biggest problem or frustration in order to snag viewers and make it clear that you're specifically addressing them.

Video Tip on getting attention: www.bit.ly/tip-attentiongrab

Question 2
How do I engage viewers so they'll want to hear me out?

Here's a bit of sales psychology: as soon as a person crosses the initial 7 second marker and makes the decision to listen, you've bought yourself a further 30 seconds of attention. This is when you must convince them that you have something relevant to them, either by revealing a solution or by dazzling them with your knowledge of the problem.

Gary Halbert, the legendary copywriter, once said that if you can describe a customer's problem better than he can describe it himself, he'll immediately accept you as an authority and hang onto your every word.

Question 3
How do I make them take action right there and then?

At this stage, the viewer will realize that:

- You are specifically addressing them
- You actually have something relevant to say and
- There could be benefits to following your advice

Now you need to present the solution and focus on the benefits—after all, the viewer needs a vision of how this product or service will profit them. As we established earlier, a cartoon is the perfect medium to convey a vision as opposed to a detailed "grown-up" picture.

The viewer needs a vision of how this product or service will profit them.

A cartoon is the perfect medium to convey a vision as opposed to a detailed "grown-up" picture.

Once you've given the viewer a vision of how they can use your product or service to their benefit, you must **clarify the action you want them to take.** This is referred to as the Call-To-Action.

This may seem simplistic, but you'd be surprised how many people overlook this critical element! The easiest way to achieve this is by just stating what viewers should do next: click this button, search Wikipedia, take out your credit card, etc…

Video Tip on calls to action: www.bit.ly/tip-actioncall

FROM THEORY TO PRACTICE

Let's turn the above theory into action using a script I wrote to promote PowToon to startup companies.

The principles are 100% transferable to any other business, and you can follow the steps to create a script for your product or service using the same guidelines.

Our evaluation of the script should be structured as a conversation between you and the viewer's subconscious:

To illustrate what I mean, this icon will be used to represent my voice

and this icon will represent the conversation in the viewer's head.

Challenge #1
Convince the viewer you're talking to him

Tip: Be direct, don't try to cover all the bases. Say outright who you're speaking to. If your viewer considers himself among this group, then he'll listen up; if not, then your product isn't directed at him anyway.

STEP 1 - ESTABLISH THAT YOU ARE TALKING TO "ME"

The viewer must be convinced that he's actually the one you're speaking to. In my case I am speaking to an entrepreneur who is trying to get his Startup off the ground:

PowToon for Startups Script: So you've got this amazing idea that's going to make you the next Bill Gates...

Conversation in viewer's head: Yeah, you know what, I do have an awesome idea that I'm trying to get off the ground. I'll give you 30 seconds to convince me that you have something that could work for me.

We now have the viewer's attention and he's given us a shot at convincing him...

Now the conversation in his head moves on: Why should I listen to you as opposed to any of the hundred or thousand others vying for my attention?

To convince him that we offer something relevant, we need to either demonstrate that we have a great deal of experience in the subject matter or show a clear benefit of the product or service.

Example:

- A nutrition expert "Isn't it tough to stick to your diet when you see all these delicious things around you?"

- A laundry service "Your washing machine takes ages and is noisy..."

- A heartburn medication "Couldn't sleep again last night because of heartburn?"

Challenge #2
Fuel viewers' interest

Tip: Start your story with a common problem among your target group.

STEP 2 – POINT OUT THE PROBLEM

PowToon for Startups Script: But every investor you pitch to fails to understand why your Big Idea is so unique. You try to explain all the important details, but their eyes just glaze over.

Conversation in viewer's head: Well, I have to explain my product somehow, and I have a pretty compelling story...what do you want me to do?

Challenge #3
Convince the viewer that you have something relevant to say

Tip: Indicate that you have a solution to the aforementioned problem or that you have some special expertise.

STEP 3 - INDICATE THAT YOU HAVE A SOLUTION OR THAT YOU UNDERSTAND THE PROBLEM REALLY WELL

PowToon for Startups Script: Here's the thing: The instant you start talking to an investor or customer, their inner stopwatch starts ticking... And you've got 90 seconds max before they completely write you off! Is there some magic way around this mental roadblock?

Conversation in viewer's head: What? They write me off after just 90 seconds? Surely you're exaggerating!

We've now created curiosity...

Challenge #4
Show the benefits of using your product or service

Tip: State the benefits of your solution—because that's what your customer is paying for! He ain't paying for the pretty packaging...

STEP 4 - PRESENT YOUR SOLUTION AND ITS BENEFITS

PowToon for Startups Script: You better believe there is! Because you're watching it right now! It's called a PowToon--a simple, super engaging way to keep investors' and customers' attention throughout your entire pitch.

PowToons translate your pitches into dynamic short animations that easily connect with your audience, showing them exactly why your business deserves their attention--and their money!

And if they want further proof that you're a savvy business owner, just let them know you created an incredible video pitch for 2% of the cost it would've run you to outsource to a professional animator or studio.

Conversation in viewer's head: Sounds like this could offer me something valuable. What do you want me to do now?

Challenge #5
Get the viewer to take a step in your direction

Tip: Don't underestimate the power of telling someone what to do. Don't be ambiguous and don't give too many options – ideally only one call to action.

STEP 5: INDICATE WHICH ACTION YOU WANT THE VIEWER TO TAKE

PowToon for Startups Script: So sign up today and bring out the awesomeness in your business!

Conversation in viewer's head: Better check this out! This might be just the thing I need to convey my message in a better way.

We've now told the viewer what he should do. Whether he'll follow-through is up to him and depends on how compelling the pitch was, but at least he heard us out…

This concludes our script!

We now have the raw material to create our animated clip. You can review the entire script in table-form in the Appendix.

Super Easy 5-Step Script Writing Recipe – Case Study: PowToon for Startups

Challenge	Step	PowToon for Startups Script	Conversation in Viewer's Head	Visuals
Grab viewer's attention and convince him that you are talking to him	STEP 1: ESTABLISH THAT YOU ARE TALKING TO "ME"	So you've got this amazing idea that's going to make you the next Bill Gates… 15 Words	Yeah, you know what, I do have an awesome idea that I'm trying to get off the ground. I'll give you 30 seconds to convince me that you have something that could work for me.	Guy scratching his chin thinking – then he has an idea and becomes happy.
Fuel viewers' interest	STEP 2: POINT OUT THE PROBLEM	But every investor you pitch to fails to understand why your Big Idea is so unique. You try to explain all the important details, but their eyes just glaze over. 30 Words	Well, I have to explain my product somehow, and I have a pretty compelling story…what do you want me to do?	Whiteboard with flow chart and Guy explaining. Investor getting bored.
Convince the viewer that you have something relevant to say	STEP 3: INDICATE THAT YOU HAVE A SOLUTION OR THAT YOU UNDERSTAND THE PROBLEM REALLY WELL	Here's the thing: The instant you start talking to an investor or customer, their inner stopwatch starts ticking… And you've got 90 seconds max before they completely write you off! Is there some magic way around this mental road block? 39 Words	What? They write me off after just 90 seconds? Surely you're exaggerating!	Stopwatch ticking while Guy is talking. Guy gets punched after 90 seconds. Guy is dejected.
Show the benefits of using your product or service	STEP 4: PRESENT YOUR SOLUTION AND ITS BENEFITS	You better believe there is! Because you're watching it right now! It's called a PowToon-- a simple, super engaging way to keep investors' and customers' attention	Sounds like this could offer me something valuable. What do you want me to do now?	Guy is surprised. Zoom out to reveal that Guy is part of a

We will now develop this script into an awesome animated video.

In Part 3, I use the PowToon software for the purpose of creating my animated video, but please feel free to use any animation software that you feel comfortable with, the principles are 100% transferable.

You'll see the finished product (including voiceover) at the end.

PART 3

How to create an awesome animated Video: An easy 6-step Process

Step 1 - Write an awesome script or short story

In this case, just grab the script we created in Part 2, or go to the Appendix and fill in the blanks on the 5-Step Script Writing Worksheet to create your own draft script.

To recap - Your script should cover the following bases:

1. Make it clear who you are talking to
2. Point out the problem
3. Indicate that you have a solution and/or expertise
4. Present your solution and clearly show its benefits
5. Call-to-action

Once we have our short story, we turn it into a script by dividing it into scenes and thinking of potential visuals that could go with it – we call this process storyboarding.

Step 2 - Storyboard

Create scenes and try to think of visuals to go with them

It does not have to be perfect at this stage! The visuals should act as the emotional support to the words; so if we talk about "confusion," an image of a confused guy can be powerful.

In my case, initial thoughts go like this:

SCENE 1

VOICEOVER	VISUAL
So you've got this amazing idea that's going to make you the next Bill Gates…	Guy scratching his chin thinking – then he has an idea and becomes happy.

SCENE 2

VOICEOVER	VISUAL
But every investor you pitch to fails to understand why your Big Idea is so unique. You try to explain all the important details, but their eyes just glaze over.	Whiteboard with flow chart and Guy explaining. Investor getting bored.

SCENE 3

VOICEOVER	VISUAL
Here's the thing: The instant you start talking to an investor or customer, their inner stopwatch starts ticking… And you've got 90 seconds max before they completely write you off!	Stopwatch ticking while Guy is talking. Guy gets punched after 90 seconds.

SCENE 4

VOICEOVER	VISUAL
Is there some magic way around this mental roadblock? You better believe there is! Because you're watching it right now!	Guy is dejected. Guy is surprised. Zoom out to reveal that Guy is part of a PowToon.

SCENE 5

VOICEOVER	VISUAL
It's called a PowToon--a simple, super engaging way to keep investors' and customers' attention throughout your entire pitch.	Show PowToon editor.

SCENE 6

VOICEOVER	VISUAL
PowToons translate your pitches into dynamic short animations that easily connect with your audience, showing them exactly why your business deserves their attention--and their money!	Text to show benefits of using PowToon.

SCENE 7

VOICEOVER	VISUAL
And if they want further proof that you're a savvy business owner, just let them know you created an incredible video pitch for 2% of the cost it would've run you to outsource to a professional animator or studio.	Guy sits at this computer creating a PowToon and is very satisfied with himself.

SCENE 8

VOICEOVER	VISUAL
So sign up today and bring out the awesomeness in your business!	Text describing the call to action.

That's the baseline to our visuals drafted. Once we have all the individual scenes on screen, we can review them and decide whether we need to add anything.

From this point onwards, we will be interacting with the PowToon software. All you will need is a free account, so please get yours here if you don't already have one: www.powtoon.com

Step 3 - Voiceover Guide / Background Music

It may seem counter-intuitive to start with the voiceover instead of the imagery. It's only natural to think: "I'll do all the visuals first, and then I can time my voiceover to coincide with what's happening on the screen" - but in reality this is a recipe for headaches.

When you record a voiceover of your script, you get much more accurate timing of the final story versus choosing the visuals while basically guessing the timing (and having to retime everything later).

Your personal voiceover is called a "scratch track"; so don't worry if it sounds scratchy and unprofessional. We just want something basic for now since we're doing this mainly as a TIMING GUIDE.

After you have done your scratch track, we can easily take the script and send it to a voiceover artist on www.fiverr.com who will get us an awesome result for between $5 and $20 for up to 120 seconds of voiceover.

For now, just do this yourself to get the timing guide.

Tip: It's much easier to record the voiceover, get it right, and then time the visuals to the story.

Ok - so we need to either choose a background track for our music or record a voiceover guide (or both).

This means we need an MP3 file of the TEXT PARTS of the script read out as they will appear in our cartoon.

Let's get started by going to the Sound Manager in PowToon and recording our voice.

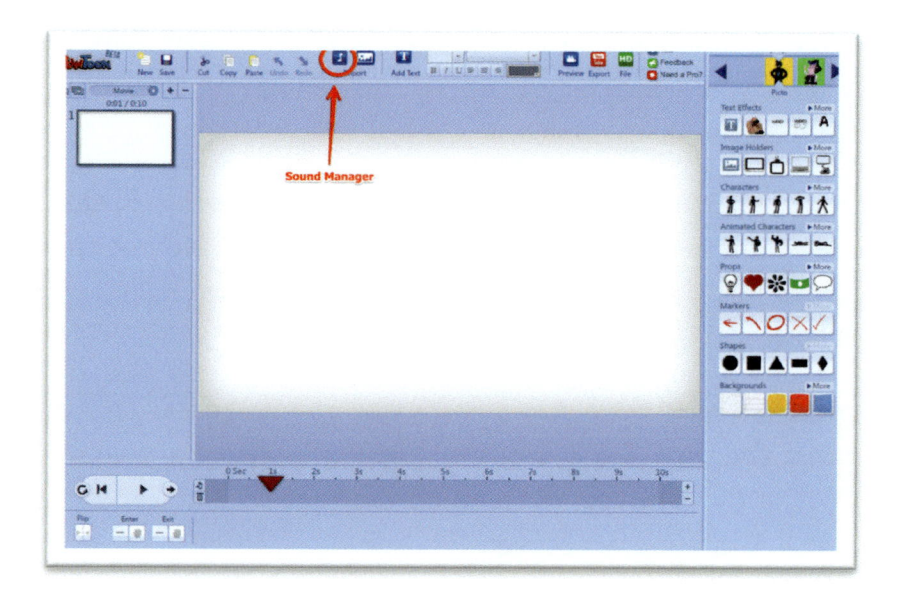

Once the sound manager is open, you can either upload (import) an MP3 that you recorded earlier, or you can record one yourself right now by clicking the record button.

Don't worry about making mistakes or getting the voiceover to sound professional; that's not the aim here (remember, for now this is more of a timing guide).

Here's the interface you'll see when you open the sound manager:

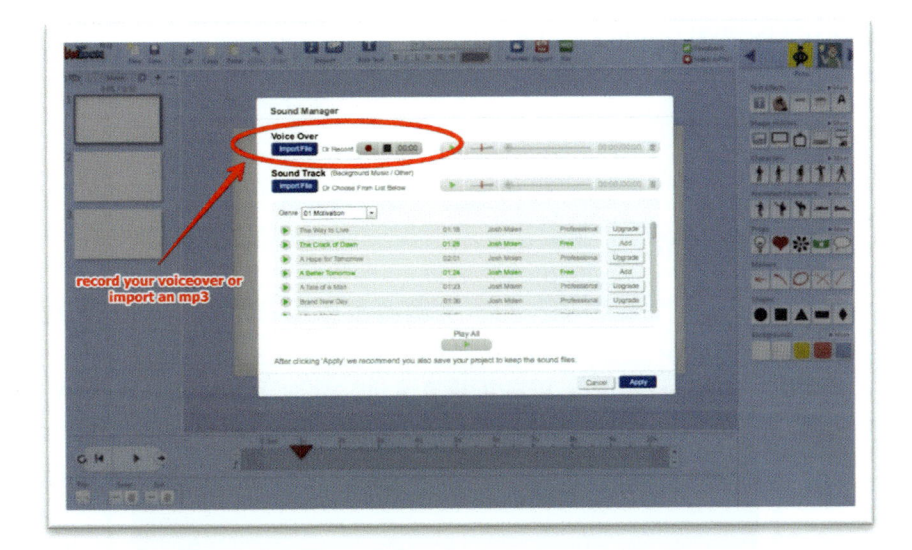

[Screenshot of Sound Manager interface with annotation "record your voiceover or import an mp3" pointing to the Voice Over section]

You can record and re-record as many times as you like. Every time you record a new version, it will overwrite the previous one.

The sound manager further allows you to choose a background track from the provided sound track list, and lets you import a second MP3 track of your choice (to stay fair to artists, please only use licensed or creative commons music). You can also regulate the volume of the voiceover and the background track separately in the dashboard to get better results.

If you would like to record and edit a voiceover or soundtrack outside of PowToon and subsequently "import" it, then here's a tool I absolutely love and strongly recommend! It's free,

Step 4 - Dividing the Slides
Slides are Scenes

Creating a PowToon is a little like directing a mini-movie. Every slide in your PowToon represents a scene that you have to equip with the right sound and visuals.

In Step 3, we created a scratch track (rough voiceover) to go with our PowToon, our next step involves creating enough slides to accommodate the sound track.

PowToon's default slide length is 10 seconds and you have a + / - on the side of the timeline to lengthen or shorten it. Each slide in PowToon is limited to a maximum of 20 seconds.

The reason for this limitation is that staring at the same scene for longer than 20 seconds in a short clip may become a little tedious. So this is PowToon's way of gently nudging our users to shake things up a little! Change the visuals if you don't want your audience to fall asleep.

Now to the practicalities:

Let's assume we have a voiceover that is 97 seconds long. We'll start with 10 slides (10 seconds each, making a total of 100 seconds).

Adding Slides

You add or remove slides by clicking the + and - in the slides panel. In our case we click + ten times.

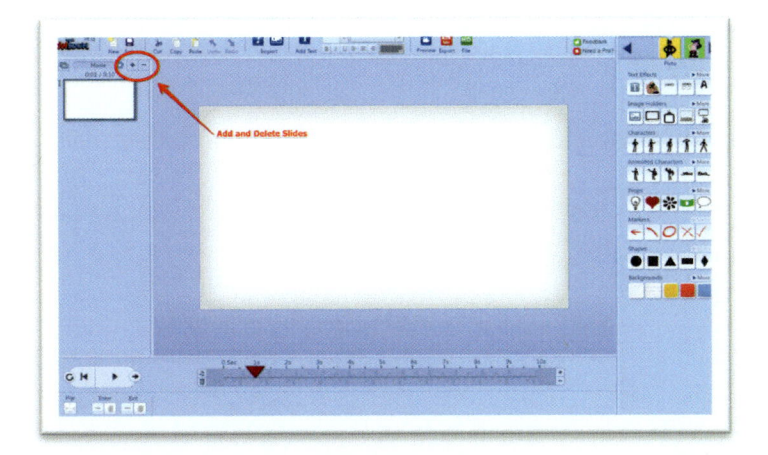

Your PowToon Editor will look like this once you're done. 10 empty slides.

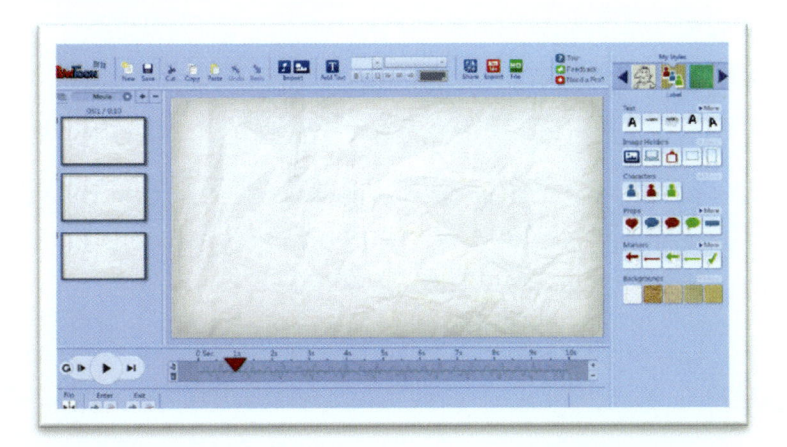

Clicking on any one of the slides will show you the timeline specific to that slide. Pressing Play will - at this stage - just play the sound track of this isolated slide since there are no visuals yet.

CREATING SCENES - Fitting the Sound to the Slides

TERMINOLOGY: Okay, we have to spend a moment on proper terminology. We're dealing with a short video here; this means we're creating a series of scenes.

There are three elements to each scene:

    1. The voiceover (or sound track): What's being said?

    2. The visuals: The emotional and visual triggers.

    3. The timing: When things happen - and for how long.

So the way we create a scene is by matching our voiceover with the appropriate visual and timing the whole thing to work together seamlessly.

Our first step in this process is to adjust the length of each slide to fit the actual length of the scenes we envision. That's actually the reason for the timing guide (or scratch track) that we created in step 2. It allows us to get our basic timing right.

For this purpose, we are going to listen to the whole voiceover from beginning-to-end inside PowToon and adjust the length of the slides to work with the voiceover.

Let me take this opportunity to introduce you to PowToon's Play Controls.

PowToon Play Controls

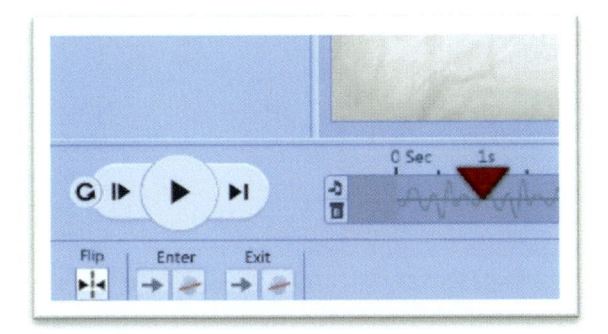

Play: play from the playhead until the end of the entire PowToon or until you pause

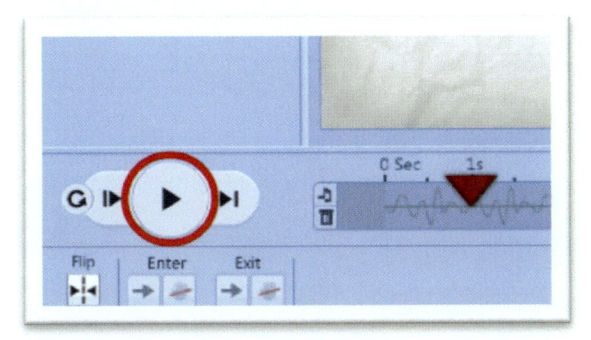

The Play button will play from the red, triangular playhead, right through to the end of the PowToon or until you stop it by clicking Pause. This allows you to see how several scenes work together.

The playhead indicates where you are on the timeline. In the above image, the playhead is on second 1 and moves through the seconds when you press Play.

Pause: pause or stop

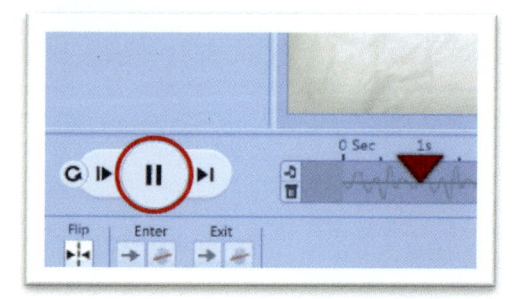

The Play button turns into a Pause button while it is playing. You can pause the PowToon at any time by clicking this button.

Play Slide: play from beginning of this slide until the end of this slide

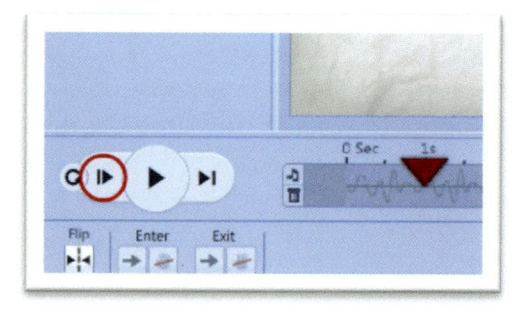

This button saves you the trouble of having to drag the playhead to zero every time you want to review the scene you are working on.

Play to Slide End: play from playhead until the end of the slide

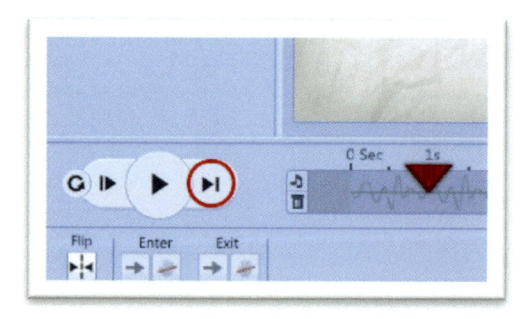

You mainly use the Play to Slide End button while working on one particular slide because it will stop at the end of the slide without moving to the next.

Play All: play entire PowToon from the start until the end

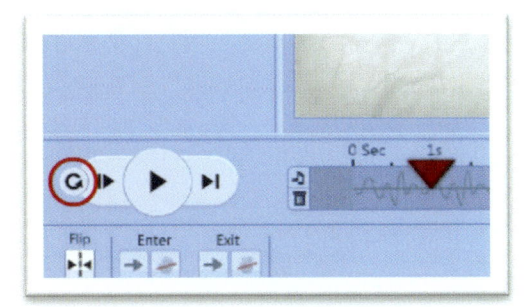

This button goes back to the beginning of the very first slide and plays right through to the end of the PowToon, or until you click pause. This is useful when you want to review the work you have done so far.

I'm sorry to go all technical on you, but there's one more thing I need to show you before we can do the fun stuff. The timeline.

The Timeline

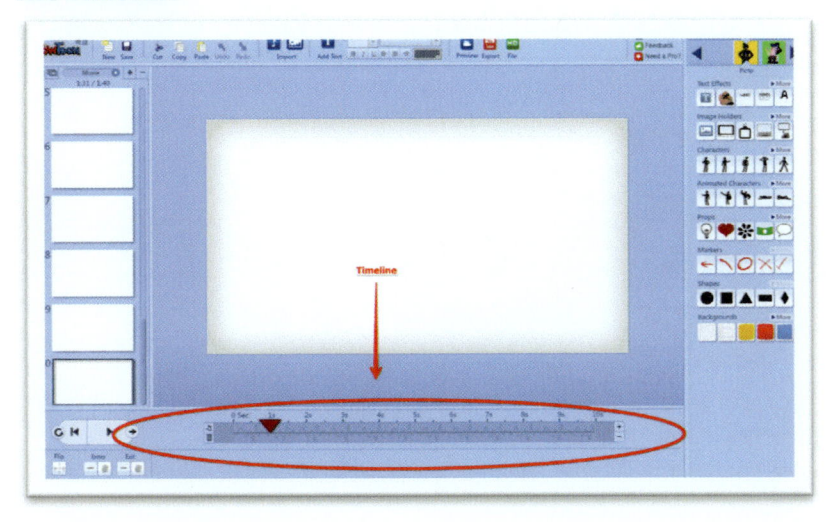

The timeline indicates the length of a slide and as the red triangular playhead moves along, it also indicates where in the time sequence we are.

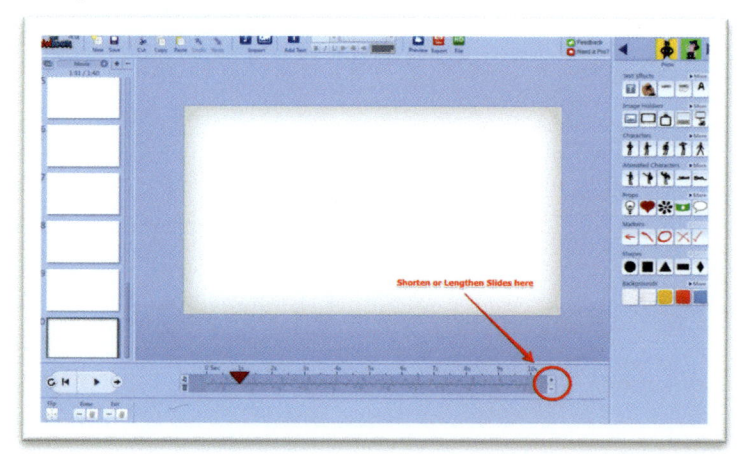

If you want to lengthen or shorten a slide, you have to press the + or - on the right hand side. The default slide length is 10 seconds and you can lengthen it to a maximum 20 seconds and shorten it to a minimum of 1 second.

Dividing the voiceover into scenes
Now we have all the tools to divide our voiceover / timing guide into scenes.
The best-practice way of dividing the voiceover is by using the following buttons.

Step 1: Press Play

This will go through all the slides until you press pause.

Step 2: Press Pause

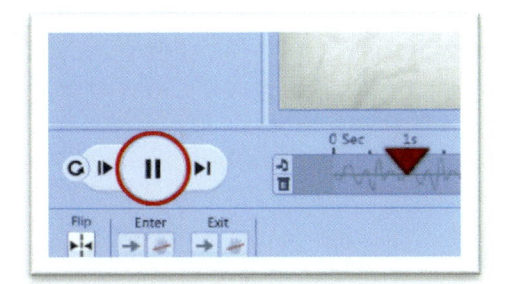

Pause the playback once you figure out where the cut off point for this particular scene is.

Step 3: Press +/- Slide Length

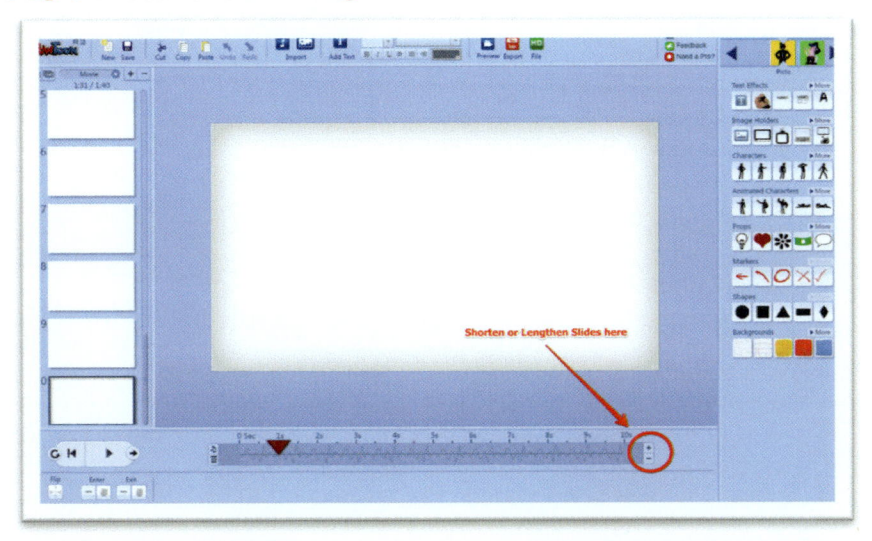

Add or delete seconds to match the voice timing. You will find the voiceover continuing on the next slide once you have finished.

Step 4: Rinse and Repeat

Move on to the next slide and repeat steps 1 through 4 until your voiceover is distributed across as many slides as you need. Fitting the voiceover into the various slides, this is how my script turned out:

SCENE 1

VOICEOVER	VISUAL	TIME
So you've got this amazing idea that's going to make you the next Bill Gates...	Guy scratching his chin thinking – then he has an idea and becomes happy.	5s

SCENE 2

VOICEOVER	VISUAL	TIME
But every investor you pitch to fails to understand why your Big Idea is so unique. You try to explain all the important details, but their eyes just glaze over.	Whiteboard with flow chart and Guy explaining. Investor getting bored.	11s

SCENE 3

VOICEOVER	VISUAL	TIME
Here's the thing: The instant you start talking to an investor or customer, their inner stopwatch starts ticking... And you've got 90 seconds max before they completely write you off!	Stopwatch ticking while Guy is talking. Guy gets punched after 90 seconds.	12s

SCENE 4

VOICEOVER	VISUAL	TIME
Is there some magic way around this mental roadblock? You better believe there is! Because you're watching it right now!	Guy is dejected. Guy is surprised. Zoom out to reveal that Guy is part of a PowToon.	9s

SCENE 5

VOICEOVER	VISUAL	TIME
It's called a PowToon--a simple, super engaging way to keep investors' and customers' attention throughout your entire pitch.	Show PowToon editor.	7s

SCENE 6

VOICEOVER	VISUAL	TIME
PowToons translate your pitches into dynamic short animations that easily connect with your audience, showing them exactly why your business deserves their attention--and their money!	Text to show benefits of using PowToon.	12s

SCENE 7

VOICEOVER	VISUAL	TIME
And if they want further proof that you're a savvy business owner, just let them know you created an incredible video pitch for 2% of the cost it would've run you to outsource to a professional animator or studio.	Guy sits at this computer creating a PowToon and is very satisfied with himself.	13s

SCENE 8

VOICEOVER	VISUAL	TIME
So sign up today and bring out the awesomeness in your business!	Text describing the call to action.	5s

Now I have the length of all my slides coordinated with the voiceover. I know the length of my individual scenes and can move on to the next stage, which is to add the visuals.

Step 5 - Populate the Slides with Visuals

This is the stage where we add animations, graphics, background, props, images, and characters to our slides/scenes.

To harness the power of toon at its maximum, we want to convey the message with as many graphic images and as little text as possible, so the audience doesn't have to sit there reading all the time (unless this is the effect you're after) and doesn't get overwhelmed with information.

Images are a powerful conveyor of emotions, so if a character is sad, it's enough to display him/her in a sad pose without adding any text at all.

An effective way to use text is by bringing individual words to life by making them appear in time with the voiceover. Only use words that can be "emotional triggers" to emphasize your message.

PowToon has a large library of characters, poses and props that you may want to use for this purpose:

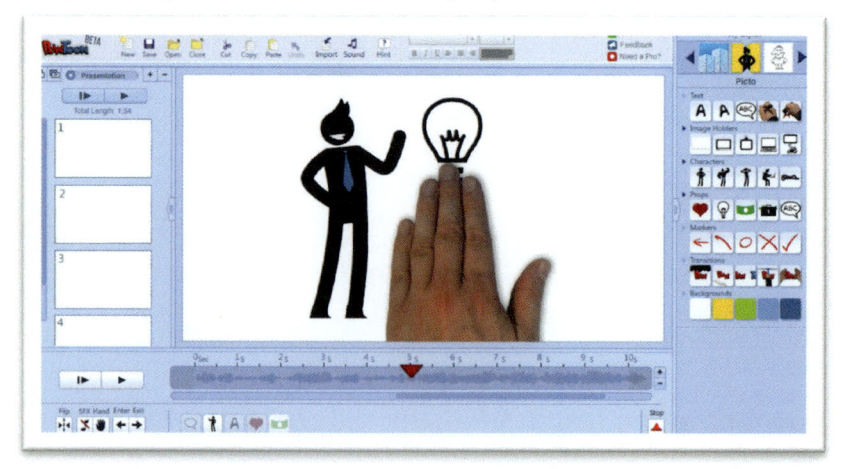

Some of PowToon's Styles

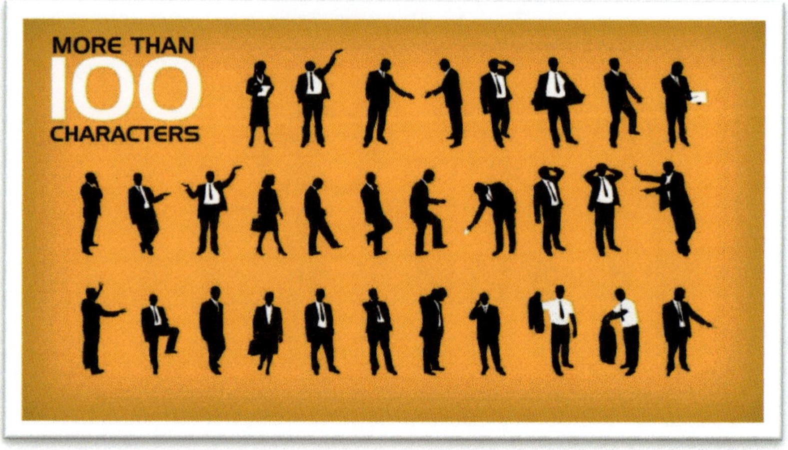
MORE THAN
100
CHARACTERS

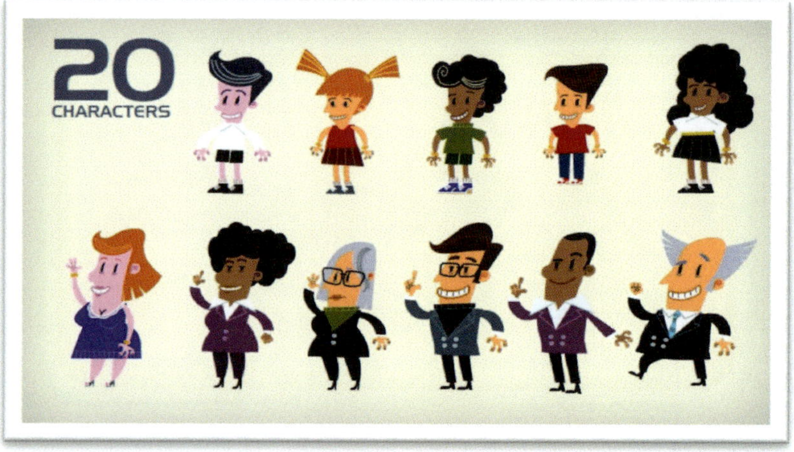
20
CHARACTERS

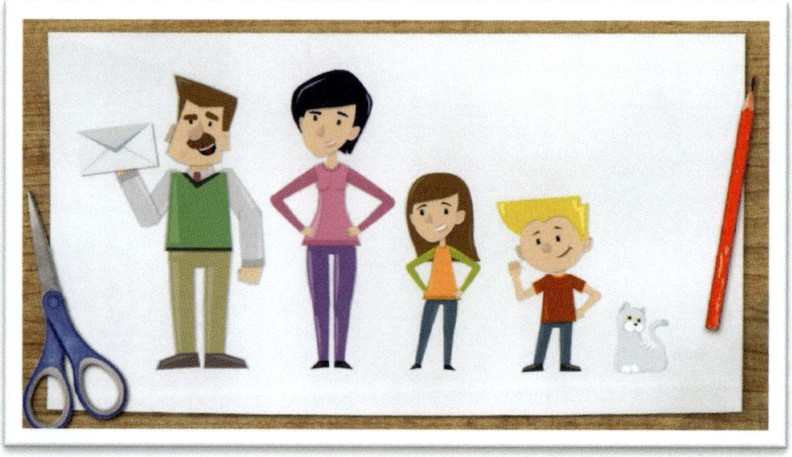

You can easily bring your own images into PowToon by clicking the "Imagine Import" icon:

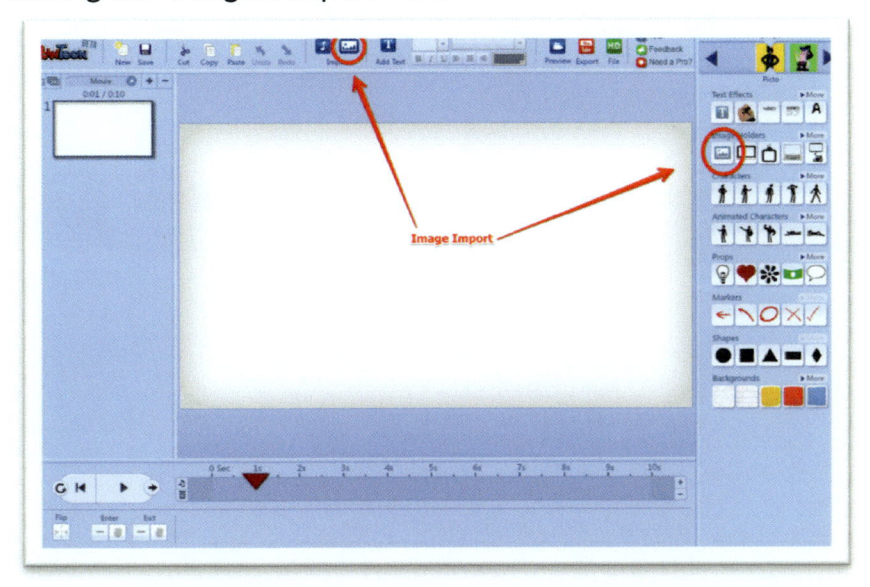

For my "PowToon for Startups" script, I chose the Marker Style. I could've made it more colorful using one of the other styles, but I really like the minimalism of this style which also works really well with photos of real people, an element I want to use in this PowToon.

Marker Style
Image Holders
Characters
Props
CREATED USING

Constructing the scene:

I'll walk you through the construction of my first scene and give you access to the PowToon template to see how to do the rest.

You can find the template in PowToon's Promotional Video > Start Ups section when you launch the PowToon editor.

SCENE 1

VOICEOVER	VISUAL	TIME
So you've got this amazing idea that's going to make you the next Bill Gates...	Guy scratching his chin thinking – then he has an idea and becomes happy.	5s

Description: I would like a "Thinking Guy" to be brought into the scene at second 1 scratching his chin. Then "eureka!" A light bulb appears and he becomes super happy.

Style

Step 1: Go to top left to choose a style. This will open the style library with all the characters and props. Choose the marker style.

Library

Step 2: Open the **animated characters** section and chose the "Thinking Guy" - you can either click him or drag him onto the screen. The character will appear on the screen and a duration bar will appear in the timeline starting wherever the playhead was located.

Duration Bar

Step 3: Now "Thinking Guy" is on the screen and we should look at the duration bar to see when he enters and exists. In this case, he arrives on the screen at second 1 (where the playhead was originally located) and leaves at second 7. You may have notices the blue triangle on the left side of the duration bar: This indicates that there is a half a second entrance effect, and looking at the symbol, the up arrow indicates that the object is brought into the screen from below.

Effects Indicator

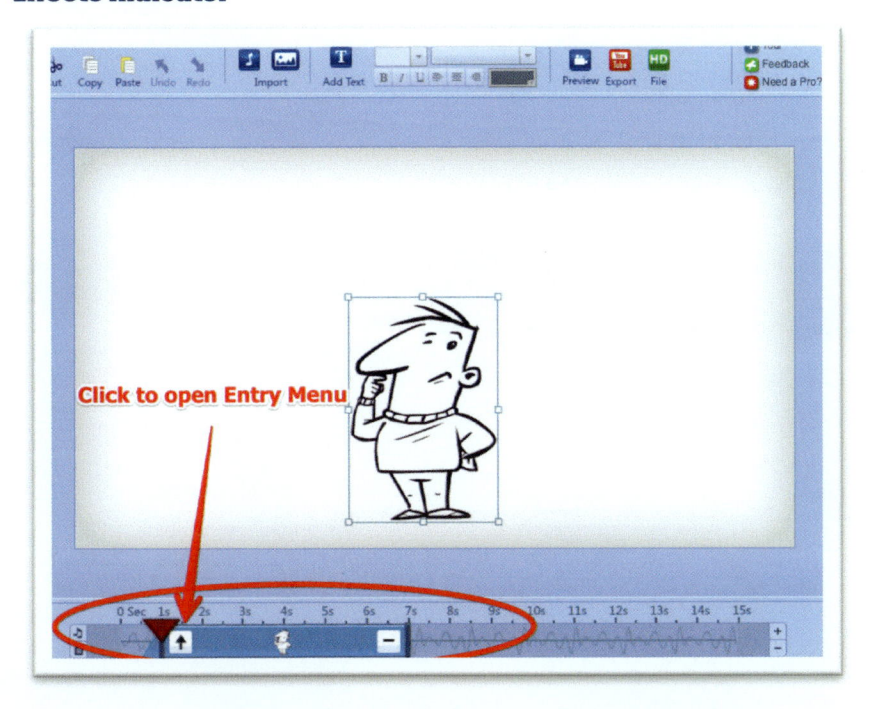

To change the entrance effect, click on the symbol and the "Effects Menu" pops up.

Effects Menu

The effect menu allows you to choose which entrance effect you want this character to have.

Handy - PowToon's Magic Hand

The effects menu also allows you to choose whether you want the object to be brought in using "Handy," our clever little hand.

Step 4: Choose an entry and exit effect for the object and adjust the length of time the object remains on screen by dragging the duration bar's ends.

Let your voiceover guide your timing, it allows you to accurately assess when an object arrives and leaves the scene.

In my case I want a light bulb to appear and the character's pose to change to "happy." This switch-over from one pose to another is best achieved by overlaying the two images and making the old image disappear while the new one appears.

This is how it's done:

We've already assigned the "From Below" and "Handy" effect to "Thinking Guy's" entry; now we assign the "No-Effect" to his exit, which means that he will just disappear once his duration bar ends. We now shorten the duration bar to end at second 2. Which means that the character is scratching his chin for 1 second (from sec1 to sec2).

Now we drag the "Happy Guy" character from the "animated characters" library section to the scene - place him directly over "Thinking Guy" and set the duration bar to start at second 2. We assign a "No-Effect" to the entry which means that as "Thinking Guy" disappears, "Happy" appears.

Now all we have to do is adjust the length of Happy's duration bar to end at second 5 and give him our chosen exit effect.

Voila! That's our main character taken care of.

But we forgot one thing.... We wanted a light bulb to appear to indicate that our Guy has a great idea.

The voice guide indicates that the right time for this is at second 3. So we drag the light bulb from the Props section and adjust the duration bar to "Pop-In" at second 3.

We have our first scene!

Review the steps we took to create the first scene:

1. Drag "Thinking" into screen - Choose entry/exit effect and adjust duration bar

2. Drag "Happy" into scene - Choose entry/exit effect and adjust duration bar

3. Drag "Light bulb" into scene - Choose entry/exit effect and adjust duration bar

I know it took a few pages to explain, but in reality our first scene should take us less than 2 minutes to complete!

Okay, now you have to do the same for scene 2, scene 3 and so on, populating the slides and timing the images. We aren't aiming at perfect matches between voice and image at this stage, but just a rough match... we'll do the fine tuning in Step 6.

Once all slides are populated, we have the first draft of our PowToon.

The process of creating a PowToon is incredibly fun, but at the same time it forces you to be very clear about what you want to convey to your audience. This helps both you and them to really GET what you want to say.

If you stay focused, you can have your whole PowToon done in 30 minutes FLAT!

Step 6 - Timing

This last step can actually have the most significant effect on the "professional" look and feel of your final result.

Along with a professional voiceover, this is where you can really make your PowToon shine.

We go through the whole PowToon, checking that we have all the timing right and making last changes and additions.

The PowToon timeline and effects/duration bar are designed to help you easily adjust the appearance and timing of all the elements on the screen.

The icons under the timeline allow you to select any object that appears in this scene without having to scroll through the entire timeline.

So let's start off by playing the whole PowToon from the start and making notes where things don't quite match.

Play All: play entire PowToon from the start until the end

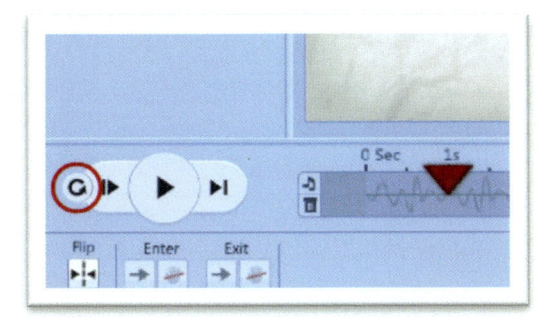

You can now listen to the voiceover running in the background and make sure that all the visual elements reflect what you hear. The more accurately you time this, the more awesome the final result!

If you get to a place where the voiceover and imagery don't match - or something is missing - hit the pause button and adjust the duration bar of the objects in question.

If you feel that the scene is too short, add the required number of seconds to the timeline.

That's it! That's how you create an awesome animated PowToon that captivates - engages - and calls to action.

A Real Insider Tip

I often get asked why we limited the time intervals in PowToon to full seconds, so that you can only place objects one full second apart, rather than 1/4 or 1/2 seconds, for example.

To answer this question, I must get a little philosophical:

When we set out to create PowToon, we wanted to build a tool that enables non-technical, non-design people to achieve exceptional, creative results. Granted, we didn't aim to replace animation or design studios, but we did have a vision of empowering any user to achieve really awesome results— results typically unattainable without flash software knowledge, design skills, or animation abilities.

So we needed to equip PowToon with many of the basic building blocks of design and animation, and make them so seamless that they appear almost non-existent. They needed to be an unnoticeable part of the landscape, so they would not distract from the actual task at hand; that of creating an awesome video clip.

For example: Handy – PowToon's helping hand - may seem to be just a hand that is attached to an object, but in reality there's a complex background algorithm that smoothes the entry and exit of the hand and creates a realistic path so the motion doesn't look robotic or strange. It's the same with every other object within PowToon – the greatest effort has been made to make the design and animation hurdle disappear.

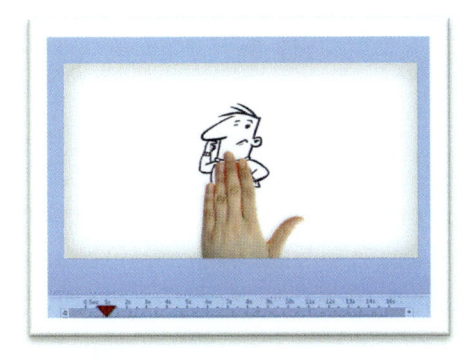

At the same time, limitations had to be set that would stop people from getting frustrated by indecision or confusion. The full second interval is one such limitation.

In the beautiful words of Antoine de Saint-Exupery (Author of The Little Prince)

"In anything at all, perfection is finally attained not when there is no longer anything to add, but when there is no longer anything to take away."

We've made the effort to take away as much as possible so that our users can simply concentrate on getting their messages across in the best way possible…

Now it's up to you to go and create something awesome!

By the way – here's the finished: PowToon for Startups Video

Follow this link to watch "PowToon for Startups" Clip: www.bit.ly/finished-powtoon

IS THERE A SHORTCUT?

If this whole process is too complicated or cumbersome for you and all you want is a great animated video or presentation without the hassle of doing it yourself...then I can tell you that you are not alone. In fact we anticipated that at PowToon! Although we don't encourage it, we recognize that many people would just like to have an animated video created for them at an affordable price, rather than the usual $2,000 to $25,000 it can cost.

If you would like a PowToon, but don't have the time or the energy to make one yourself, you can have someone create a PowToon for you (or your business) for around $400 - $700. Just go to the PowToon Studio and ask a professional for help: www.powtoon.com/studio

They will write the script, arrange the voiceover, and create an awesome PowToon for you.

Here are some examples of what Master PowToonists from the PowToon Studio have created.

www.bit.ly/studio-01

www.bit.ly/studio-02

www.bit.ly/studio-03

Whether you become a PowToonist yourself or hire a Master PowToonist to create one for you, we wish you happy powtooning and much success in your business!

A Personal Note from the Unicorn

I put a lot of effort into the writing of this book in the hope of giving you a tremendous amount of value.

Thank you for accepting this gift and making the most of it.

In the spirit of giving you huge value, I have included a special link to a bonus exclusive to the book readers.

http://www.powtoon.com/cartoonmarketing/special/

Much success and happy powtooning

Ilya Spitalnik

PowToon's Chief Unicorn

P.S. I would love to hear your thoughts and comments on the book, please write directly to me: ilya@powtoon.com

About the Author

Founder and CEO of PowToon, Ilya Spitalnik is an internationally recognized thought leader, keynote speaker and advisor on best business practices in the Google Era.

His passion for entrepreneurship inspired him to leave a successful career in banking to concentrate on building startup enterprises across numerous sectors including real estate, information technology, software and energy.

Alongside his deep marketing expertise gained from hands-on roles in dozens of online projects, Spitalnik has developed a proprietary Vision Selling™ methodology which empowers non-sales people to master the art of closing a deal in an ethical way.

His most recent venture PowToon, an animated presentation software company that gives anyone the ability to easily convey their message in a dynamic and powerful format, has grown to 235,000 users in its first year of operation. Powtoon embodies Spitalnik's vision for tech solutions that truly make a difference in both the personal and professional arena.

You can contact him directly at ilya@powtoon.com

Appendix

Super Easy 5-Step Script Writing Recipe – Worksheet

Challenge	Step	Your Script	Conversation in Viewer's Head	Your Visuals
Grab viewer's attention and convince him that you are talking to him	STEP 1: ESTABLISH THAT YOU ARE TALKING TO "ME"		Is this guy talking to me? Is this content addressed at me?	
Fuel viewer's interest	STEP 2: POINT OUT THE PROBLEM		Oh I recognize this problem….	
Convince the viewer that you have something relevant to say	STEP 3: INDICATE THAT YOU HAVE A SOLUTION OR THAT YOU UNDERSTAND THE PROBLEM REALLY WELL		Why should I listen to you? Do you have a solution for me? Do you have any personal experience with the problem? Are you an expert in the field?	
Show the benefits of using your product or service	STEP 4: PRESENT YOUR SOLUTION AND ITS BENEFITS		What is the benefit for me using this product or service? What's in it for me?	
Get the viewer to take a step in your direction	STEP 5: INDICATE WHICH ACTION YOU WANT THE VIEWER TO TAKE		Ok where do I pay, sign up, or find out more about this?	

Super Easy 5-Step Script Writing Recipe – Case Study: PowToon for Startups

Challenge	Step	PowToon for Startups Script	Conversation in Viewer's Head	Visuals
Grab viewer's attention and convince him that you are talking to him	STEP 1: ESTABLISH THAT YOU ARE TALKING TO "ME"	So you've got this amazing idea that's going to make you the next Bill Gates… 15 Words	Yeah, you know what, I do have an awesome idea that I'm trying to get off the ground. I'll give you 30 seconds to convince me that you have something that could work for me.	Guy scratching his chin thinking – then he has an idea and becomes happy.
Fuel viewers' interest	STEP 2: POINT OUT THE PROBLEM	But every investor you pitch to fails to understand why your Big Idea is so unique. You try to explain all the important details, but their eyes just glaze over. 30 Words	Well, I have to explain my product somehow, and I have a pretty compelling story…what do you want me to do?	Whiteboard with flow chart and Guy explaining. Investor getting bored.
Convince the viewer that you have something relevant to say	STEP 3: INDICATE THAT YOU HAVE A SOLUTION OR THAT YOU UNDERSTAND THE PROBLEM REALLY WELL	Here's the thing: The instant you start talking to an investor or customer, their inner stopwatch starts ticking… And you've got 90 seconds max before they completely write you off! Is there some magic way around this mental road block? 39 Words	What? They write me off after just 90 seconds? Surely you're exaggerating!	Stopwatch ticking while Guy is talking. Guy gets punched after 90 seconds. Guy is dejected.

Challenge	Step	PowToon for Startups Script	Conversation in Viewer's Head	Visuals
Show the benefits of using your product or service	STEP 4: PRESENT YOUR SOLUTION AND ITS BENEFITS	You better believe there is! Because you're watching it right now! It's called a PowToon - a simple, super engaging way to keep investors' and customers' attention throughout your entire pitch. PowToons translate your pitches into dynamic, short animations that easily connect with your audience, showing them exactly why your business deserves their attention - and their money! And if they want further proof that you're a savvy business owner, just let them know you created an incredible video pitch for 2% of the cost it would've run you to outsource to a professional animator or studio. 95 Words	Sounds like this could offer me something valuable. What do you want me to do now?	Guy is surprised. Zoom out to reveal that Guy is part of a PowToon. Show PowToon editor. Guy sits at this computer creating a PowToon and is very satisfied with himself.
Get the viewer to take a step in your direction	STEP 5: INDICATE WHICH ACTION YOU WANT THE VIEWER TO TAKE	So sign up today and bring out the awesomeness in your business! 12 Words 191 Words	Better check this out! This might be just the thing I need to convey my message in a better way.	SIGN UP NOW!

Printed in Great Britain
by Amazon